Cautery

Aaron Brossiet

Chapbook Press

Schuler Books
2660 28th Street SE
Grand Rapids, MI 49512
(616) 942-7330
www.schulerbooks.com

Cautery

ISBN 13: 9781966196334

Library of Congress Control Number: 2025923492

Copyright © 2025 Aaron Brossiet

Cover art by Aaron Brossiet – Self-portrait (2021)

Printed in the United States by Chapbook Press.

For my family: past, present, and future.

"Improvement makes strait roads, but the crooked roads without Improvement, are roads of Genius."

— **William Blake**

Part I

The Parsonage	1
Cracked China, Broken Bone	2
Long Gone, Never Gone	3
A Poet Who Serviced a Church Clock	5
Death Pass	8
To Face the Fire	9
Dirty Mouth Deb c. 1974	10
Summer After the Divorce	12
Ars Poetica #790	14
Tradition	16
Body Full of Holes	17
What's On Tonight	18
Boyhood	20
Nova	22
Lost in Translation	24
Pottawottamie Indian Preaches	25

Part II

Industry of the Body	28
The Drink We Never Shared	29
Multipath	30
Ice Fishing	31
Bird Hole	32
Sweeping Up Broken Glass	33
Spoken Like a True Shadow	34
Cold Nipples	35
Garden of Earthly Delights	36
Murmuration	37

This Is Supposed to Be   38
What Ivor Thord Grey Would Say   39
Bardo   41
Nobody Fathered My Blind Eye   42
Rabbit X   43
Where Accidents Happen   44
Easter Sunday   45
Crazy Horse Resurrected   46
Postmortem Questions for My Dad   47

Part III

October   49
My Fading   53
The Wild One   54
The Point of It   55
Spring Music   57
Through the Dead Trees the Moon Shines   59
Adam and Eve   60
To Do List   61
Sorrow Will Cool   62
Ingleside   63
Drawn in Blue Pencil   64
Over the Hills & Far Away   65
This Bread is My Flesh   66

The Parsonage

At the kitchen table with porcupine
quills lodged in his gums,
      my father types his sermon.

      I scamper wild, skinned for stew.

My mother drowns the two heads
of a blind snake in a barrel of wine.

      Summer heat
      and a dozen marbles
      hidden in my mouth.

Cracked China, Broken Bone

There were Air Force reserve pilots rupturing the sound
barrier directly over our house, cracking the China, plates
& cups, in the hutch.

There were sunflowers weighed down by September
snow & our Samoyed named Pasha, Lara's younger lover
in *Dr. Zhivago*.

There was my fear of massasauga rattlesnakes slithering
in my tractor tire sandbox & wandering aimless & lost in
the green husks of cornfields.

There was excitement in my veins when my dad's church
was robbed. (And grown-ups following tire tracks to the
trailer of Kenny's dad).

There was my dad lying on the couch with a broken
ankle, an eggplant between calf & toes, too much to
drink, leaning and peeing in a Jif Jar.

Long Gone, Never Gone

is the smoke —
the aroma of Captain Black

tobacco. What the mind chooses
to resurrect cannot

be tethered to a chain
in the backyard. Why

the afternoon he tilled the garden
emptying mouthfuls of blood

into the soil and not the day the kittens
heaped together in a cheap football helmet?

Tonight, I remember my father
taking his father and my brother,

and me—fishing—the dogfish
flopping in the bottom

of the aluminum boat, echoing
across the entire bayou. I don't

recall stepping into the boat, or
rigging my line, but here and now

I feel the sun burning on my neck
just after lunch. Maybe

my father already had his vodka
on, or maybe he forgot the stringer. But

the fish continues to pound and suffer,
gills snapping open and shut.

My grandfather takes the stem

of his pipe, like the handle on a hammer,
and beats the fish upside the head,

in a rage rivaling the fire of the sun,
until blood leaks from the fish's eyes.

A Poet Who Serviced a Church Clock
My father's life as a Joseph Cornell box

I spy him crouching on his knees with a rock raised high
above his sobbing eyes directly over a tiny yellow
deformed baby duck. Its neck curled like a lowercase n,
its vision of the world upside down. Beaver Island, on a
summer afternoon in 1981.

Grandma dropped a nickel in a canning jar every day for a
year to donate to John Birch.

Always the smell of pipe tobacco as he would lurk. He
said he put the duck out of its misery behind the
boathouse.

After his Easter sermon, my father sat across the street
from us eating bread, each bite soaked in red wine.

The weather in my father's box is always the cornucopia
of November under steel grey skies.
The John Birch society labeled Eisenhower a Communist
dupe.

Beaver Island, on a summer afternoon in 1981, he reclines
across the street smelling of pipe tobacco.

Firing up his pipe, my father took his seat at the kitchen
table in front of his manual typewriter surrounded by piles
of books, thick books, heavy books, serious books. No
fiction. Books written by men attempting to understand,

explain, or justify their ideas regarding *Our Father Hallowed Be Thy Name. Our Father Who Art in Heaven.*

After the John Birch society labeled Eisenhower a Communist dupe, Grandma plopped two nickels in the canning jar every day for a year to donate to J.B.

Alone with waves and bolts of lightning, he feels at ease with his piles of books, thick books, heavy books, serious books.

If the typewriter keys no longer produce the words to soothe the fire in his soul he stands up, and slides his chair away from the table, and rambles toward his sons with tears in his eyes, with sadness due to the pending dead leaves of his life; he stumbles toward us to hold us. Chest pressed to chest we can feel each other's heart beat.

Eisenhower — Communist dupe.

In his desk drawer I unearth a postcard of a bird like Julie Christie, elbow cloaking her nipple under steel grey skies.

In his dreams he never abandons the lighthouse.

He bellows his sermon from the cylindrical pulpit high above the water. Next to him a picture of a bird like Julie Christie, elbow shadowing her nipple, but exposing the rest of her breast.

My father would tiptoe toward us. His box. His
resurrection Easter.

In his dreams he never surrenders the lighthouse. Instead
he sits at his perch listening to the wind roar and the
waves pound against the pier. Alone with waves and bolts
of lightning, he seals his eyes.

A hawk flies out of a birch. Always the cornucopia of
November.

The statue in my mind is him crouching near the fireplace
on his knees with a rock raised high above his sobbing
eyes with Julie Christie posing naked in the background.
Our Father Who Art in Heaven.

Our Father Hallowed Be Thy Name. Our father who art in
heaven no longer births the words to extinguish the fire.

He slides his chair away from the table, and crawls
toward his sons with tears in his eyes, with sadness due to
the pending dead leaves of his life.

A bird like Julie Christie naked.

Julie Christie Julie Christie Julie Christie a bird Julie
Christie Julie Christie Julie Christie writhing Julie
Christie Julie Christie Julie Christie storms Julie Christie
Julie Christie Julie Christie pounding Julie Christie Jesus
Christie Julie Christ Jesus Christie.

Death Pass

Never would my grandfather dream
of the mountains of mail-order catalogues

or Catholics honoring a gypsy, isolated
from the news in a basement full of snakes.

To Face the Fire

In the dark she places her hand
on my shoulder, her mouth near
my ear, she whispers my name
so my little brother, sleeping in the
next bed, doesn't wake. In the middle
of the night, he is a burr bouncing
super ball thrown hard against
the wall. I wake and she holds
my hand and leads me down
the dark stairs, past the vodka bottle
on the coffee table, and my father asleep
on the couch and into the kitchen.
Sitting on the table in the nook,
we watch the Shooks' barn burn
in the distance. The colors orange
and yellow dance a terrible pumpkin
dance raging to life. The bones, studs
& joists, of the barn, look skinny
compared to the expanding
fat flames. The leaves on nearby
trees rattle away in the winds of heat.
Tiny flames stay to the ground and
crawl outward across the property
like small waves crashing against
Lake Michigan's shores. Exiting the
barn's mouth a horse gallops out
of the inferno, its mane and the rope
around its neck an orange signature
across the starless black night.

Dirty Mouth Deb c. 1974

I sleepwalk outdoors at night
     and kneel at the homemade
    grave
placing my ear to the ground.

My husband is riled and ashamed
         of his death.
While fixing the hinge
      on the hatch
at the top
    of the silo,

(as the corn poured down
      from the vertical elevator)

he slipped and fell into
     the two-story statue of a bullet.

Autopsy showed it wasn't the fall

     that killed him.

His windbreaker acted like a parachute
    and brought him steadily down.
     But nobody could hear him
and two tons of corn that followed

    like rain

    collapsed both of his lungs.

Each night, at the grave

I   place   handfuls
     of dirt
    in each pocket
and one in my mouth.

Summer After the Divorce

The older boys in the neighborhood would punch us with
rhino head fists, middle knuckles raised— its horn—in
the thighs until we no longer could walk.

Devoured piles of kidney beans and ground beef, lucky if
it included small pieces of translucent onions.

Popped a wheelie on my Evil Knievel bike in front of our
duplex and the front wheel kept
        rolling down the sidewalk.

My mother shimmied in a Vegas-Esque performance at
        the high school auditorium. Her costume
Caribbean water and headpiece blue feathers.

Along with his six-pack he purchased a tin of chew for us.
The tobacco conveniently sealed in tiny teabag-like
pouches.

On Thursdays, before he would deliver us to a pizza, my
dad would mow the lawn even though he no longer hung
his pants in our closets.

My mother smoked cigarettes, cried, and stared out into
the backyard until the middle of the night.

She left a note for us that our Samoyed was escorted to
the farm.

Swindled a kid out of his Joe Namath rookie card and found my body shaking when my friend put me in a Chinese finger trap.

We learned to swim out of an undertow, not against it. This was true even away from the beach.

Listened to the neighbors shoot hoops in the evenings. Started conceiving my escape.

Discovered that after a while we all wash our dreams with wine and our hands with turpentine.

Burned the rule book, then the Bible, so I could see where I traveled in the dark.

Ars Poetica #790

Men would saunter through the front door and eat pea
soup at the kitchen table with me. When full, they'd flee
out the back-

door. I claim only one beautiful mother, but at the card
table of my wandering mind, I was dealt a royal flush of
daddies.

One of my daddies suffered a gnarled ring finger fighting
a rabbit that struggled to stay out of the crock pot.
Crouched behind home

plate in the third inning, another daddy busted his thumb
in four places. Never looked to the dugout. Healed
crooked, his finger.

Didn't stop him during timeouts from pinching my
stomach until it bled. He taught me to stand still and stare
up at the rafters.

My daddies! One daddy fell asleep in the woods and
dreamt he was a wolf. Another daddy rolled a '72 Dodge
Charger

fleeing the over under double barrels of an angry cuckold.
That daddy married a movie star. And lost her. One daddy
taught inside

a trailer during the day and baked Toll House cookies for
dinner. What's yr daddy do? My daddies stood behind
the pulpit, stormed

the sidelines, mowed the lawn weekly, drank gallons of
vodka, got hooked on heroin, and lost some teeth. In the
end, they all wound up

on their knees and weeping buckets at my beautiful
mother's feet.

Tradition

In a dark box
one rabbit at a time
snatched from coop
to the cardboard pen.

The .22 barrel is a steel snake.
The bullet its poisonous tongue.

In the dark box, the rabbit eyeballs
the snake in the mouth and waits.

Body Full of Holes

With snake shot in his .22 my father cratered hundreds
of holes in the rat snake: a scarlet constellation

in a body like a black garden hose. Dead
crow on the deck this morning, on the shovel's

steel blade it is soft and light. At times I'm mute
to my own attacks. I only know what I'm working

by trusting not knowing what I'm working. Tonight
I play my fiddle standing on the ribs of the beast.

The lady in my woods is the seed, the root,
and the flower to the ailing animal that is me.

What's On Tonight

My mother's B & E took place when owning
a color T.V. still remained outside the monthly
budget before President Carter stood
at the podium ramrod and tied the P.L.O.
to the Ku Klux Klan. Earlier that fall,
the Dodgers slammed into the magic
of Reggie Jackson, who stitched wings
on baseballs to fly over centerfield walls.
The year Rick James deserted the Mynah
Birds to soar solo, and Charlie's Angels
perched in my dreams. That winter my dad
drove across town to shack with his dad.
His new woman living five or six red lights
down the road in a neighboring town. I think
she rented a green aluminum-sided house.
It's hard to articulate because by the time
my mom told me and my brother to button
our coats and tie our shoes, it was dark outside
and parked in the other woman's driveway, engine
idling, heat blasting, our heads sleepy, Mom
          let herself in
and I watched her silhouette shadow through
the picture window, shadow slashing
across the drawn drapes. As my brother
began to wake, I told him to glance
out the rear window, look at the dog,
circling and peeing on the snowman
with the pipe in his mouth. We crumpled over
cackling; we crumpled over crying. As my mother

drove back to our skinny duplex, I leaned over
the front seat, and whispered,
I am proud of you letting the words settle
like snowflakes, and then we made pancakes
for dinner and cruised the channels on T.V..

Boyhood

My mom coos for me
from the backdoor
to say goodbye. I hide
on my belly in the grass
where I am a plastic army
figure with no face,
Jessie James on the lam,
the Bionic Man. I spy
on her exit. She is wearing
a turquoise dress and eyeliner
to match. The curl in her
hair fresh as a birthday
ribbon. She says goodbye
to Hope, my sitter, and skips
down the walkway smiling
and taking the offered hand
of a man I haven't met.

He opens the door of his Trans
Am, stands over her as she slips
in the passenger seat and shuts her in.

Where is my walkie-talkie
with my dad on the other
end? And my dog who moved
with him when he left? I need
my baseball bat, or the rifle
used to butcher the rabbits. Or the
grenade my grandfather found

marching through Bernay. Or
my great grandfather's axe
that back in the day took care
of that undisciplined ox.

Hope calls me to dinner,
but I pretend not to hear
her. I'll return after
she wipes the grease
off the stove and then
make my demands for dinner.

When the evening moves
from Honolulu blue to
Coca-Cola black night, I will
hide in my mother's bed
staring at the buzzing street light
outside her bedroom window
until I hear her return
and Hope drive away.

Nova

Even with the windows down, the humidity and my
father's cigarillo smoke take up a stubborn occupancy in
the car. Sitting in the backseat, with my two brothers, I
feel like I am covered in licked sucker and the smoke
feathers my hair and embroiders itself into my Pistons t-
shirt. On the radio the Tigers are playing the California
Angels and Alan Trammel is up to bat.

From my position behind the driver's seat, I can see out
the front window, and to my left out my back seat
window. The rearview window is blocked because the
trunk is wide open, stuffed with two sandy inner-tubes
from our day riding the waves of Lake Michigan.

Just past Pfaff's Pharmacy, only a couple of blocks from
my father's house, we spot a woman inch her bare feet
down the three front steps of her duplex. She is heading
toward her sprinkler on the edge of the sidewalk. She is
tall and lean with skin the color of a glass of milk
splashed with coffee and long black Rita Coolidge
straight hair. Her bikini is yellow.

Just out of eighth grade, I have had my share of awkward
make out sessions, a handful of breast touching
experiences and one painful night of blue balls. My dad
slows the car down. This beauty is rare like spotting a
pair of albino deer or seeing the Aurora Borealis. I sit up
and stop breathing. My dad glides the car past her yard.
Too soon, I can't see her out my window.

Suddenly, he stops. A week before, wandering barefoot in the marble corridors of the State Capital, my father's impulsive nature earned us an escort out of the building. He puts the car in reverse and accelerates backward at a steady clip. I can see her again through my window. My body is charged with electricity from my belly to my toes.

To move her sprinkler without getting wet she stands on the sidewalk with her back to the road. Her long body bends forward toward the sprinkler, hair hanging almost to the ground. Her breasts nearly slip out from her top. In my mind, no more dad, no more brothers crowding me in the backseat, no more sidewalk or sprinkler, smoke or humidity, only pitch black and her glowing yellow bikini bottom lights the night sky of my world.

She spots us gawking, stands up straight, spins around and glowers.

My dad opens the driver's side door, ashes his cigarillo, and reaches deep under the body of the car. He pulls out a silver dollar which he holds between two fingers toward our super nova bikini clad lady. Must be my lucky day, he yells to her. She smiles, turns, and with a bounce in her step, moves the sprinkler closer to the bush below her porch. My dad shuts the car door, drives on, and Trammel rounds second into a stand-up triple.

Lost in Translation

Brother, do you remember the older girl, the one who volunteered
as a Candy Striper that mom said was a gentle soul?

The girl who used to bring us chocolate milk and apricots,
the one who refused to give away any of the kittens.

Once she feed me mint leaves. Some days you & I used
to sneak down the road to spy on her singing while

she collected eggs. Her voice was water receding
through shells and rocks on the shore. I no longer

remember her name. I do remember that every
house harbors sad stories. The memory of her is like

that day mom hung sheets out to dry on a September
morning but they froze instead in the frigid air. Later

that day, wet snow clung to sunflowers weighting
them down, until they bowed humbly to the wind.

Pottawattamie Indian Preaches

a sestina

October fog lurks over the goose-pimpled river.
Just us. Me, my brother, and dad.
Huddling with cigars dad snaps a match. We circle on the
fire.
Standing in earth's cold sweat our boots heavy with mud.
The river hums dad his sermon
and sings to my brother and I about Indians.

Stories of Pottawattamie Indian
summers and prayers given at the mouth of the Grand
River.
Dad's eyes swim in his sermon.
A swallow perches on a cattail. *Should I shoot it dad?*
He nods and smiles at my immature bravado knee-deep in
mud.
The gun breathes its fire.

Dad's eyes reflect the fire.
Shotgun bells ring funeral songs disturbing ancient
Indians
and I wish I would be swallowed by the mud.
I beg God to say something and the bird alive, but even
the river
won't speak to me. We stare at death: me, my brother,
and dad.
Dad digs the bird's grave while he thinks of words for his
sermon.

At the podium, in the basement, dad sculpts his sermon.

Outside my brother and I melt army figures with fire.
I whisper to him *only with a sense of humor will you*
understand dad.
Then we shapeshift into Geronimo and Crazy Horse and
sing Indian
songs. Time will never erase the river,
and the bird is forever buried in the mud.

Images of that day—caked behind my eyes like mud.
I don't remember a single sermon,
but I'm haunted by the lesson learned at the river.
I sit watching smoke fade above the fire
listening for the truth from the ghosts of Indians
and pondering about the dreams that afflict my dad.

I don't want to be haunted like my dad,
but some things just can't be buried in the mud.
I wait for the Indian.
I listen to the sermons.
I stare into the fire,
but the truth is the secret of the river.

In my dream, the Indian preaches the sermon.
My father finds peace knee-deep in the cool mud
and the fire burns inside the river.

Part II

Industry of the Body

Symptoms

This–

    Body wakes in flight

This–

    Body looks over the rocks sewn in its shoulders
    For the ever-present threat of a blaze

This–

    Body's heart beats like a bag
    Of worms

This–

    Body checks & rechecks its own trending:
    Burning tire cinched around the lower back

This–

    Body believes clean up is impossible
    In a world full of unlimited bombs

This–

    Body is exhausted of itself, but
    Knows no other body as well as its own

This–

    Body desires
    So many bodies other than its own

This–

    Body imagines your body

This–

    Body imagines being in your body

This–

    Body houses a tongue

This–

    Body's tongue sings

The Drink We Never Shared

Unexpectedly, my father lifted
up his hospital gown. I glimpsed,
hanging between his thighs,
sagging and stretched, his purple
boxers.

On the chair beside me, his cane hangs
off the back. His hand seeks this stick
and he loses his balance. He leans into me

and whispers *did you bring her?*

Across the room, my denim jacket hangs
on the hook. It lives on
that hook. I take the bottle out,
grab two cups off the counter,
and bring her back to the table. Muted
on the television the Angels
battle the Pirates. World
Series and nothing changes.
Wind and freezing rain buckshot
against the nursing home's window.
At the table we drink our whiskey,
avoiding the words that should be dealt.

Hear the heavy roaring
as the storm rolls away.

Multipath

The morning that repeats itself is the one
where the beet juice bled from the red flannel
hash into your butter-drenched rye toast.

As I sit across the table from you, I watch
your eyes run rivers that also bled beet.
You lift your bandaged left hand out

from under the table — the result of waking
up and attempting to stop the naked blade
of the fan. Again, I threaten to mail-fist

you sober. The more I understand the hole
you shoveled out of yourself, the tougher
it is for me to redeem the momentum

of your departure. The foozle rhythm
of your years on the planet beats uneven
in my ears through the static reception of days.

Ice Fishing

Cutting holes into
Long Lake's winter crust,
a world hard
as the edge of a tooth,
my hands plunge deep
inside the icy water
fishing for God.
I want to grab God
by the ears and pull
her through the tiny hole
to a star-filled sky
full of whys.

Bird Hole

Through my windshield, red-wing blackbirds perch on
                    telephone wires above
soggy ditches and cattails. Yellow, red,
          & black feathers, colors of my father
cremating. Another red-wing
          blackbird dogfights a green darner
dragonfly too big to swallow.
     In its beak, thorax cracked,
the fight & flight is over.
Since he died, a bird
     lives in the center of my
          rib cage thrusting its wings in vain. To
exhaust my bird,
          drown my bird, I tried. Considered putting
a bullet in my bird. Instead, I
     imagine my bird as a hole in the sky, behind
which is an alley, my
     escape. In the paper, people are reported missing
every day.

Sweeping Up Broken Glass

Of course there is none near / the pool or its dressing
rooms. / Material unwillingly pulverized from its original
/ form is always more interesting. Our best stories have
jagged edges. The butcher's floor — / spotless. A ninth-
grade girl wrote that her stepfather / taught her to draw
when she visited him in prison. He served seven years /
for his involvement in a drive-by. On the sidewalk / no
glass. / Instead a mouse belly up with rain-matted hair.
Another student / wrote that when her father left she was
told / he was on a golfing trip. Two years later he showed
/ at the doorway of her second-grade classroom /
unannounced. Tears / are a form of broken glass, / as well
as gasps for breath. / It's a shame we hide our shards of
days. / We should wear them as jewels in our crowns.

Spoken Like a True Shadow

Shadows of branches boogie in the breeze
across the pavement outside my front door.

Poems in boxes, poems in bottles,
poems in police reports— always a new bird's

egg to be hatched or cracked. Too tired to
climb this mountain, too far to turn around.

How is it possible that I feel both raw
and cooked? Sunburned and frostbitten?

Let me stand on the kick drum and clap my
hands. Let me stay under the sheet from

head to toe. Help hoodoo me, mumble
some mumbo jumbo, scramble me numb.

Cold Nipples

Too many months since I've glimpsed
the moon or whispered to a woman
in a mini-skirt. Stray cats don't even drink

the milk I leave them at night while
I wander the streets, a drunken
beetle. In Chinatown, I beg Dr. Lau

to prescribe love tea. He fingers my pulse
and speaks in Chinese. His resplendent
daughter translates, "You have weak heart."

Cornering love? More difficult than catching
crows on my tongue. On the sidewalk, a lady
shakes her cup—three quarters & a dime.

She howls, like a wolf toward the moon, as I
eye a younger woman wearing a t-shirt
and jeans, jaywalking against the biting wind.

Garden of Earthly Delights
After Hieronymus Bosch

A book of Flemish & Dutch paintings splayed open on
my floor; Images of the Christ child & the Madonna's
nipple on my floor.

Animals symbolizing the deadly sins, with horrible genital
organs spewing torrents of fire and darkening the earth
floor

with mud. Though I'm still in town my mind is already in
Memphis. Under a disco ball, Isaac the Murderer and
Lady X grind on the dance floor.

Oh, where did the nights go when we could satisfy our
love & lust naked and hidden in the beach grass with only
a blanket and sandy floor?

In the morning, the murmuration of swallows spells their
story; the papyrus on which it is recorded—shadows on
the Southern sky.

Murmuration

Over boiling rapids:
black starlings cloud
and undulate in patterns:
mottle on Petoskey stones:

black cherry stains: my
white shirt, traces of lips:
movement of your mouth.

This Is Supposed to Be

an ode to a girl wearing red
shoes, but it got fucked up
along the way by reports
of pink slime supplementing
our ground beef like packing
socks in your crotch to add
girth to your limp meat. Then
a Presidential candidate
yacks it up in the Sunshine State
about building colonies on Mars
while someone shoots a black kid armed
with his Skittles & an iced tea. Because
we don't wear guns in rooms where
teenagers learn, my state Senator
says I am working in the last mass
murder empowerment zone.
Then my aunt leaves a note
& dies. In a home. Not her
home. She writes, "No visitation.
No memorial. Just think of me."
Which I am, though I'm also
thinking about the girl in the red
shoes, & what she did to save
that three-legged dog dodging
cars in the street. But then Carlos
tells me Fabian was jumped. He
says this giggling. His brother.
Broken orbital. He points to his eye.
Broken cheekbone. Splattered nose.

What Ivor Thord Grey Would Say

My Dutch relatives don't understand the Spanish
bandied about El Elegante barbershop, or why

Los Dias de Muertos is celebrated at Cesar Chavez
Elementary. They stare at their shoes instead

of validating the young *Ponch "o" Villas* hanging
outside the doorway of Canita's hip-hop store. They
pound

Budweiser at the bar, Coctailz, which advertises
POLASKI DAYS & FREE POOL. Aunt Isla

used to toe the line on these curbs during Memorial
Day parades and sculpt dough into palm-sized windmill

cookies every day of the week. The '57 Chevy is still
wedged into the lobby of John & Sons Used Cars

and Body Shop. Dutch names linger on neighborhood
signs: Sommerdyke Plumbing; Van Raalte and Tulip
Streets.

Ivor would warn, *borders lead to vulnerability* as Island
Latinos keep the bus stop bench between themselves

and the Mexicans. Ivor would prophesize. *Beware
amigos,*
just past the Dollar Store and Four Star Gas,

*Taco Bell gringo managers keep the drive-thru
open to assimilate & satiate hungry bellies late into the
night.*

Bardo

for Adam Yauch

I never fret about the sun setting too early,
or celebrating my birthday on the 4th of July
rather than the 5th of November. Day after

day burns off. Year after year the sun shines,
leaves turn orange, snow falls, flowers bloom.

When I sported my baseball hat cockeyed
and my sleeveless t-shirt soaked in
cheap beer, *fighting for my right to party,*
I never saw the similarities between the boom

box and the shape of your gravestone. I never
dreamed your exit from the stage could take place

before your daughter's doe eyes burned with her
own rebellion. In my dreams I am unable to erase

your face from the cover of Rolling Stone. I imagine
you with Monarch wings taking flight with the wind.

Nobody Fathered My Blind Eye

I can't even smell the onions on my fingers,
as I wipe the tears from my cheeks. Nobody
asked me where
I shoplifted my suit of skin, tonight's dented armor;
or delivered me his supererogatory
opinion on the menace of men wearing hoodies while
humping the street.
During the day I push my way through throngs of people;
but I pretend to live in a sealed cave.
I am so sad I can't stop laughing,
"Pull me over," I howl
though Nobody hasn't opened his ears to me.

Nobody said February snow would grow deep enough to
bury black history;
Nobody said I would never fit the description;
Nobody said this chalice from which we drink is
patriarchs' nectar.

Nobody is stationed in the control tower that
we cannot eyeball because privilege is as invisible and
ravenous as measles. Empathy my only vaccine.

I thought I had been governing myself the whole time;
setting alarms, scrambling eggs, and sizing up
the punk on the train threatening my alabaster life.
Tonight, I recognize my collective reflection
in the kitchen window, ghosts hanging in my tears,
history carving its path down the wrinkles on my face.

Rabbit X

for Gerrit

My brother pointed out the birth of a ten-foot rabbit
with X's for eyes, born from the tip of an aerosol can,
underneath the overpass, near a mini-golf course
across the street from Arby's in a town
that claims a gay-bashing diesel truck repairman
who might regret his post now
that he is up to his dirty fingernails with hate
comments that include, among other
things, the egging of his property and a personal
threat to his nuts and bolt and this morning
the discovery outside his screen door that leads to his
cellar, a bushel full of dead rabbits with X's for eyes.

Where Accidents Happen

On the shoulder of any American
highway — two pieces of wood
can be found forming a tiny cross.
A screw connecting small boards,
typically painted white; at times
stenciled with names of the deceased:
Luckey Haskins, or *Wannamaker*,
the ones no longer riding along.

At times, the memorials are gussied up
with fake white carnations frosted blue
or pink at the petals' edge. Maybe a
red ribbon looped at the intersection
of boards. At times, a soggy teddy bear
slumps at the base, head hanging, one
eye missing.

Near Bluelick, Kentucky,
instead of a cross, someone planted
a metal stake and hung wooden wind
chimes. Each time the chimes touch,
clapped by wind stirring from the velocity
of semis, hauling heifers or swine, many notes
give voice to a life ended
unwittingly in that particular spot.

Easter Sunday

Reverend Al Green suffers from infirmities and needs a little wine,
and because he is Christian he embodies many *infirmities*. God Bless the wine.

Putting my butt into a pew today is its own kind of resurrection.
Don't believe the way they taught me to believe, yet I bathe in their wine.

Two six-year-old girls, one white, one black, color together on the same
page —some crazy ass elephant wearing a birthday hat —my kind of wine.

Under a guitar signed by Othar Turner we order pulled pork in spicy
barbecue sauce, cole slaw — Mississippi pecan brown beer — no wine.

I say to myself, "Hey Beady Eye, you should've learned to play guitar."
No whine—life is fine— as long as you keep steady the pour on my wine.

Crazy Horse Resurrected

In the alley behind Neiman Marcus
Crazy Horse crawled out of my mouth.
I'm not surprised.
I've been wandering around
with a voice in my belly.

With a voice in my belly
I've been wandering around.
I'm not surprised.
Crazy Horse crawled out of my mouth.
In the alley behind Neiman Marcus.

Postmortem Questions for My Dad

Do you believe you ever penetrated the surface of a day?
How do I find my harbor if the lighthouse is destroyed?
Was your loneliness always the ocean or did you spend
    nights in the moonless desert as well?
While alive did you learn a birdsong?
When you entered the abyss what did you believe?
Did you ever find a harbor to anchor?
Like a vest on fire, how long can I wear your earthquake?
How long will I walk the fault lines of your heart?
What should I say to my son?
What do I tell my daughter?
Can the psychic silo of memory be emptied?
Is what isn't said a part of your song?

Part III

October

I.

If I stop pushing and pulling the spatula
across the cast iron pan, the pine nuts
turn the color of bark. With my daughter
sitting on my lap
staring at the computer screen, she
and I harmonize on the word "Whoa"
when the photo of the Gila monster's
cauliflower-shaped skull appears. Meatballs
in the oven make tiny popping noises
on the rack above the orange heating coil.
The wind rattles leaves down the street;
the sun dissolves slowly into Lake Michigan;
the book of poems is splayed open
on the glass table; my hand settles
between your thighs; your fingers are cold
as darkness descends on burgundy trees.

II.

A woman's teeth litter the sidewalk,
white bone bullets on dried blood; knuckle of a cop;

amid reports of another movie star flashing side boob;

amid pictures of a soldier missing a leg,
hopping on the foot still in its boot;

amid drone planes punching holes in apartment buildings
where a girl wearing a red hijab stands on a coffee can to
boil cardamom;

amid a classroom of students writing, one standing at my
desk,
assignment in hand, tears pooling in the lower half of her
eyelids; tea cups;

III.

The cat purrs near my feet;
its white bowl filled with tuna in my hands.
Other than semi-trucks migrating through
the nearest intersection, the house is silent
after the coffee machine stops percolating.
Morning remains the color of a velvet navy dress.

IV.

A weatherman points
to the animated snowflakes
over Lake Michigan;
I serve salmon with zucchini
and pine nuts;

coriander and orange
peel in wheat beer;
apparitions swing
from the birch trees;

Japanese maple drips
evening rain; I leave
the oven door open
to warm my hands.

My Fading

My reflection stares back at me
from the window as night stands
in morning's way. Outside a storm
is blowing, the trees are twisting.
Red tail lights on cars pierce black
rain. When I speak to my reflection,
his lips move with my lips. He nods
when I nod, scratches when I scratch.

The Wild One

My son cracks the cocoon
of my embrace as we lie in the bottom
bunk of our vacation cabin. It's the stones
of muscle growing in his shoulders.
A couple of years ago these shoulders
felt thin enough to thread through a hook.
He's built himself on dunes and snake
grass, pulling fish from the lake. Tomorrow
he will explode through the screen door,
letting it slam. He'll hit the dock,
legs churning, until he reaches the end,
vaulting above the water, attempting to turn
both arms into helicopter blades against
gravity's invincibility.

The Point of It

*According to the Big Bang theory, the universe
was born as a very hot, very dense, single point in space.*

Imagine the stored energy it takes kevlar to halt the bullet
from entering my chest and exiting through my spine. The
universe

is an energy bank managing constant deposits and
withdrawals.
I borrowed the energy I use to hoist the bar and plates off
my chest.

Once a basketball is in the air, it takes buffalo energy to
stop
an alley-oop, but not so much as a breath to launch the
Monarch off

the perch of my finger. If I snatch up a book, I elevate it
with energy older than
the blind poet who constructed Odysseus out of song.

Calculate the energy it takes a rocket to escape the bonds
of gravity. Imagine the energy
it would take to push the moon out of earth's orbit.

I know it requires work to scale the fire escape, only the
moon spotlighting my way.
I hope you will let me climb through your window at this
hour. It's hauntingly

too long since I felt the 80 watts of heat produced by
another human breathing near my ear. In hurricane
history, this desire is the kinetic energy of Katrina. I
imagine myself as a forest

fire, releasing heat and light through thousands of burning
trees and you the howling wind.

Spring Music

Today, the sun gives me cheer
    and I wag my tail
    and lower my ears.
Starving for blue skies teaches one to submit. Oh,
  the long-legged ladies run
  once again around the lake
      which is a teardrop stain on earth's crust.

On days like this a young man, a choir boy
  who, despite the blue skies, suffers
  from the unrequited song of
  a Puerto Rican girl
        with long notes
and peanut-butter-colored eyes.

The ice still drips from the eaves
onto the sidewalk as I enter
the market to purchase bottles of red wine,
to soften an already soft afternoon.
The black guy at the entrance,
      holding the door open, wears
a black cowboy hat embroidered
with eagles.

He hums.

Inside the butcher looks bored
    pouring buckets of ice
    onto dead sea creatures: raw

shrimp, Bluepoint oysters,
smoked whitefish, and orange
salmon filets. In the eddies of aisles

from the corner of mine eye
a Siren with waterfall-long hair
sings.

I tie myself to my shopping cart.

Through the Dead Trees the Moon Shines

Most days start *mostly cloudy* this time of year,
but a day can also open its robe
and let us peek at its blue sky
                    and daffodils.
        At my age, I can look at my
life as half over or half done. It's up to me.

Swollen buds on the tree branches protrude like spikes
on a torture stick. Yet last year's rabbit birthed
pink bunnies under the deck who are already
grown into fuzzy softballs with ears and legs. By
summer's end, the neighbor's dog will do them in.

Anyway, there is more parking at my son's guitar
lessons now that the building next door imploded
under the weight of February snow. The heel
of my shoe peels and a hole is ready to spring
near the knuckle of my big toe. It could be worse.

I thought what I wanted would shine.
I thought whiskey would taste terrible in a paper cup.
I thought life insurance would protect my survival.

When I open my car door, the hinges
scream like a fox with
its leg in a trap and a broken back,
but when I drive through the bohemian section
of town, a tattooed couple kisses on a bench in the sun.

Adam and Eve
After Albrecht Durer

Instead of painting a Mountain Ash, ancient Tree
of Knowledge, with looming snake hovering over Adam
& Eve, he parts the two from holding hands; individual
panels,

each standing their ground on scorched clay pocked with
stones, tough on tender feet. Adam and Eve stand naked
and gazing on the edge of the world with a choice.

Instead of lusting after their golden hair & perfectly
proportioned bodies, firm breasts, parenthetical hips,
strong arms and thighs, I want the black abyss, always
there in the background, waiting

At times I wish to reduce my life to gesso
and white canvas: absent of moose & cow, rabbit & cat,
absent of roof & kitchen, shirt & tie, absent of children

in need. This is the twisted apple lodged within me; a
need for silence as necessary as water; a thirst
quenched only by lowering myself, in the bucket, down

the dark well of words. A toast: to the void before us,
to the wonder and awe of the Fall, to those of us
without angel wings, to emptiness, that space.

To Do List

If in fact you
        are to die to -
night you better
start to value the moon.
        You've barely glanced
its way lately, maybe
twice in two months.
        Having not noticed,
you can only imagine
its white shadow sheeting
        the west side leaves
of the maple tree.
If in fact, you are to die
        tonight pay attention
to the subtle digging
of your son's voice
        toward the rhythm
of deep waters. Eventually,
you will recede into its
        ebb & flow as your father
did to yours.

Sorrow Will Cool

My fingers massage aloe into the scar that will never let
go of my body. This branding is a contract, a
marriage of a molten sear and skin on the field
of all my days. Do not build a fence around the burn,
rather day and night, like prayer, keep the memory clean
and one day my children will finger it. I will let
them explore the calloused bump. My
hands may tremble, lips quiver, eyes blur. My children
will question me. They will open this burning drawer
often,
and I will beat back the desire to shut
and lock the drawer on fire, the
desire to extinguish yesterdays and douse the flames.
This branding iron heated in sorrow
will cool, the embers swept away with brooms.

Ingleside
   after Richard Diebenkorn

Despite the blue sky and radiant sun,
the houses up the hill are barren
of trees abutting empty grass
land. Soon the empty space will crawl with
yellow backhoes and bulldozers, heavy
metal and horsepower caged in steel
preparing to cobble more houses, pave snaky
black streets and pour white sidewalks.
Transplanted trees stand black. But the grass
bleeds green and the houses shine bright white
with red and blue roofs. I am drawn to its
possibility.
A life of symmetry, rows upon rows
of houses all brightly lit from above. Yet
the unspoken rocks loudest. No four-year- olds
churning their legs on Big Wheels, no
middle school boys in sleeveless t-shirts
riding dirt bikes on the streets. No girls.
Nobody mowing a lawn or picking up the trash.

Drawn in Blue Pencil

I beg her to point her blue pencil at me like a wand. Long tentacles of electricity hiss from the pointy lead and bite into my flesh with molten hooks. I scream, but I tell her *don't stop. Lift me over your head and shake the salt out of the paper cuts I call wounds.* The reality is much simpler than all that. The solace of my short suffering doesn't need the spectacle of cinematic proportions. The real balm is to watch her move her blue pencil from point A to point B, and from point C to point D until the lines reveal a portrait of a man with tiny tips of hair on his head and along his jawline. A child's portrait of a father is really a map, a topographical recording of the routes he took through the mountains and valleys until his ashes float across the surface of Lake Michigan. Let the record show, the smile on his face was of the highest elevation ever recorded.

Over the Hills & Far Away
After Robert Rauschenberg's "Retroactive I"

Many are the moves
my ballerina makes, her leg
in white tights, a steeple
rising from hip, past ear
& pointing to a world
without end. These words

ring like the church bells
of my past. My father
standing behind the podium,
potato juice instead of water
in his glass, which after the sermon
will help him find deep sleep.

Through the riddle, not
the narcotics, I find myself,
far from evening's visible moon,
walking backwards with my
eyes closed on Shook's farm,
lost to dusk, the blood of strawberries.

Later, lying on my back
looking at the sky, I wonder
when did we stop dropping our
jaws at the sight of jumbo jets
releasing their white thread into
the wind and the blinding sunset.

This Bread is My Flesh

I
Sun reflects off storefront windows.
Inside the bakery, warm brown loaves slide
into plastic bags, knotted & displayed on shelves.

II
On the counter is a bag of wheat berries,
a pitcher of cold well water, and measured
half cup of sea salt, flour, and brown eggs.

III
Fingers and forearms dusted with flour
claw and push dough across
the butcher's block.

IV
Other than ingredients, the dough is
shaped in long aluminum molds, glass,
or drop biscuit pans.

V
Jesus sits with both hands on the table,
palms up. On the plate between his hands,
the bread. The disciples look away, toward
each other and whisper.

VI
As a child in church, the bread passed across
adult hands right in front of my face. A

pile of neatly cut squares on a large gold
plate.

VII
At the dinner table the loaf remains whole
until we grab it and tear it apart.

VIII
When my father eats, he dips his roll
in his glass of red wine. His
eyes bloodshot and gentle
in the waning light.

IX
He knew by morning his hands would
be bound and he would wear a crown
of thorns, but now he focused on the
bread in his mouth, flavors of honey
and salt.

X
Two empty bottles of wine on the table.
You reach across the table with a piece
dripping with olive oil toward my mouth.
The crust is tough, but the bread is wet
and warm.

XI
Standing high above the congregation,
my father would raise his arms, palms

toward the sky and say, "Unless you eat
the flesh of the Son of God and drink
his blood, you have no life in you."

XII
Crumbs on the plate. Crumbs on the floor.

XIII
This morning I serve it to my daughter
and my son, with the sweet blood
of raspberry jam, each piece resting
on the palm of my hand.

Acknowledgments

I am grateful to the editors of the following publications for publishing versions of a number of the poems in this book: The Mac Guffin, Redneck Review, Jet Fuel Review, Drunk Monkeys, Sky Magazine, Mudfish Magazine, and Forage Poetry. I also also like to thank Great Lakes Commonwealth of Letters and judge Heather Sellars for selecting "Cracked China, Broken Bone" as the winner of the 2010 Literary Life Poetry Contest.

I am forever indebted to all my professors in the M.F.A. program at the University of Texas at El Paso, especially Sasha Pimentel and Dr. Jeff Sirkin. Thank you to Amorak Huey for keeping me in the poetry game over the years as well as to all the members of the Poet's Choice monthly writing group. Thank you to my first poetry teacher and forever mentor Miriam Pederson. I am also deeply grateful to Kathleen McGookey for all her help in shaping this collection. Thank you to my parents: Mary, Ron, & Larry. To Mimi, Micah, and Amaya — Viva Love.